Written by ABHISHEK TALWAR

Illustrated by SONAL GOYAL

The Adventures of BIPLOB THE BUMBLEBEE

VOLUME 5

Published by RITIKA TALWAR

Biplob World Pvt. Ltd.

Biplob the Bumblebee: The eco – warrior superhero is the cleverest bee. Ever. He uses only his wits to solve the most difficult problems in the most natural, eco – friendly manner!

Farmer Balram: He manages the farm and garden that Biplob lives in. He is Biplob's best friend and depends on him to make sure his garden and farm remain naturally healthy.

Addy & Avantika: Two siblings who live in the city and visit Biplob's garden whenever their school has holidays.

Farmer Jaggu: He is a very rich man who has bought a farm and garden in Farmer Balram's village. Jaggu thinks that he can solve all problems with money and has very little respect for nature and the environment.

Floppy – Avantika & Addy's loveable little cocker spaniel, Floppy is a well – meaning dog, who usually gets into trouble for no fault of his. Thankfully for him, he is so cute that everyone loves him irrespective!

The Flowers: MS. Daisy, MS. Hibiscus, MS. Violet and all the other flowers in the garden keep Biplob cheerful. They're always there to help, just as Biplob helps them!

1

The 'drip – drop' answer

"I wonder when they'll arrive," muttered farmer Balram, squinting at the sun.

"Who?!" asked Biplob, jumping with curiosity.

Farmer Balram looked down surprised, "Oh Biplob, its you!"

"Yes but are you expecting a guest to drop in from the sky?" asked Biplob in jest.

"Not just expecting," replied farmer Balram, "But praying that this guest arrives in abundance."

Looking at Biplob's perplexed expression, he said, "Follow me and you'll understand."

“Look here,” said farmer Balram, pointing at the well.

“But this is nearly empty!” observed Biplob with dismay.

“We only have water to last us five days. If it doesn’t rain soon, we are in deep trouble,” nodded farmer Balram, “So that is the guest I was looking for – the rains!”

“Even with rainwater harvesting, we have fallen short of water this summer,” observed Biplob gloomily.

Next morning, as farmer Balram watered the fields, Biplob heard a cob of corn sigh, “Finally, water to quench my thirst! Pity most of it is going waste.”

Biplob whirled around, shocked. “Waste?”

“In the time the water takes to seep through the soil,” explained the cob, “The sun evaporates most of it!” Biplob buzzed towards the ground and saw that the cob was right!

"With the summer sun so hot, some water will evaporate. We can only try and save as much as we can," said Biplob.

"All I hear is excuses," replied the cob, it's eyes twinkling, "Aren't you the smart bee that told farmer Balram about rainwater harvesting? Surely you can think of a more efficient way to water the fields!" Biplob nodded thoughtfully to himself.

That evening as Biplob dried the dishes, he suddenly yelled, "Hey look!"
A startled farmer Balram saw the tap was dripping, 'plip plop, plip plop'.
"Don't yell Biplob! I'll fix the dripping tap tomorrow."
"But this dripping tap is the solution!" exclaimed Biplob, pirouetting and waving the dishcloth around like a flag! 'Poor Biplob,' thought farmer Balram to himself, 'I think he has had a sunstroke.'

"Why not have a system where drops of water fall ONLY on the roots of the plants!" exclaimed Biplob.

"Rubbish!" replied farmer Balram crossly.

"It's not rubbish," persisted Biplob, "If the water drips exactly where the roots are, it will instantly seep into the soil and won't evaporate! Instead of five days, it may last an entire month!"

"Enough Biplob!" scolded farmer Balram. Biplob reluctantly went to bed.

Next morning at breakfast, Biplob saw farmer Balram all dressed up. “Hello! Going somewhere?”

“Biplob, the rubbish you spoke last night was actually quite brilliant!” gushed farmer Balram, “I researched on the internet and found there’s a country called Israel, which is very dry. Looking at how little water they have, they invented something called DRIP IRRIGATION, a process to water crops exactly how you described.”

"Maybe they have leaking taps in Israel too," Biplob mumbled between bites.

"I don't know about that, but I am going to get everything needed for drip irrigation," replied farmer Balram.

Farmer Balram got pipes and nozzles which he connected to the well. He then laid them out across the farm. When he turned on the pump, water slowly started dripping from the nozzles.

"It works!" exclaimed Biplob. "Thanks to you Biplob!" replied farmer Balram, "Our water will now last till the rains arrive!"

"And I get a new shower!" exclaimed MS. Violet happily, as water dripped on her roots, drop by precious drop!

2

From the shoulders of Giants

“This is so boring and useless!” exclaimed Addy as they trooped into Biplob’s garden.

“But you still have to study history & science,” replied Avantika.

“Humphh,” snorted Addy crossly, “Who cares if Newton discovered Gravity? It’s not like we were floating around aimlessly while Newton scampered to find Gravity and tell us about it so we could all come back to earth!” causing Avantika to giggle.

"Children these days," sniffled MS. Violet, "Only want fun and games. Ask them to study and they make excuses!"

"Don't be rude Violet," scolded MS. Hibiscus, "Though she does have a point Addy. History teaches us what our ancestors have done, invented and discovered. We can build on that to make a better, cleaner and healthier world!"

"I think everything that had to be invented and discovered is already done," sulked Addy.

Suddenly, Avantika yelled, “Hello – these pipes are leaking!” She pointed to the pipes dripping water onto the plants. “Quick, let’s find farmer Balram and tell him!” she said, as they turned to dash back to the house – MS. Hibiscus called out to them to stop, but it was too late.

"Whoa! Where is the fire?" exclaimed Biplob, seeing them running.

"No fire," replied Avantika, "but if there was one, we wouldn't have any water to put it out!" "Really?" asked Biplob.

"Yes," replied Aditya, "All the pipes are leaking."

"Well, drink some water. Then we'll investigate these leaking pipes," said Biplob, offering them glasses of water, "After all, we cannot run out of water in case there's a real fire!"

When they returned to the garden, they bumped into farmer Balram, who beamed at them, "Have you seen our new drip irrigation system?"

"Drip irrigation?" asked the puzzled children.

Biplob chimed in, "They thought the pipes are leaking!" He and farmer Balram burst out laughing.

"Those aren't leaking pipes children," smiled farmer Balram. He explained how they had installed a drip irrigation system to save water.

Back home, Avantika gushed "Wow Biplob, you are the smartest!"

"Not really Avantika," replied Biplob, "If I have seen further, it is by standing on the shoulders of giants!"

"Are there giants here?" asked Avantika fearfully.

"No, it means I appear smarter because I read books about the wonderful things people have done. Whenever there's a problem, I apply this learning to find a solution," explained Biplob.

“But where are the giants Biplob,” asked Addy impatiently,

“Right here!” said Biplob, proffering a history book.

Seeing their confused expressions, Biplob continued, “Like MS. Hibiscus said, history is very useful. That quote about ‘shoulders of giants’ was made by the great scientist, Newton. Several scientists before him made great discoveries and inventions. That helped him in his work.”

"So, Newton meant that the hard work done by our ancestors was the 'shoulders' on which he could stand and look further than anyone else," said Avantika thoughtfully.

"Absolutely," beamed Biplob, "He was thanking and complimenting his predecessors at the same time!"

"Hmmm. Now I understand" said Addy, looking contrite. "But how do YOU know what MS. Hibiscus was telling us? You weren't there in the garden!"

"Actually, I was there, behind the roses," said Biplob, "When you left, I dashed back home and prctended I was already here."

"So, you knew what I had said about history. You quoted Newton only to teach me a lesson!" exclaimed Addy.

"Yes, after all, gravity affects you more than me. I knew I could always get back to the house before you!" answered Biplob lovingly as they all burst out laughing!

3
An Eye for an Eye

Addy and Avantika were super excited – this morning they were going trekking with Biplob!

They quickly finished breakfast and headed out with their water bottles and sandwiches. “Don’t forget your caps,” said Biplob as Floppy flapped his ears and barked excitedly. They trooped out, passing through the village as it slowly woke up and came to life.

As they passed Jaggu's house, he called out, "Ho Biplob, where are you off to this early?"

"We're going to the woods farmer Jaggu," replied Biplob, as Addy and Avantika wished him good morning.

"Forget the woods. Come in here and admire my Californian Brandywine tomatoes and Portuguese Brinjals," said Jaggu haughtily, the sun glinting off his gold tooth, "And see this, the most special Russian potatoes!"

"How strange," replied Biplob, tongue in cheek, "India grows the best Brandywine tomatoes. We're also the largest producer of Potatoes and export Brinjals to Europe, where they're called 'Aubergines'. Yet, you've imported those same plants from other countries!" as Addy and Avantika giggled.

"Impertinent bee," shouted Jaggu, angry at Biplob for pointing out his folly. "Go to your blasted woods, maybe you'll find some plants there to grow in your garden!"

"What a nasty man," said Avantika, as they reached the woods.

"Ignore him," said Biplob, "He's too full of himself."

"Look," exclaimed Addy, pointing up, "These trees are as tall as the buildings in the city!"

The sun peeped through the branches as Floppy dashed amongst the trees, barking happily as if to say, 'Hurry up!'

Biplob pointed out interesting trees and small animals as they walked.

Soon they reached a meadow with a little stream flowing through it.
"I love this spot!" shouted Addy, "Let's stop here."

They sat in the shade of a banyan tree and enjoyed the delicious cheese and jam sandwiches. Once they had eaten, Addy pulled out a ball to play 'catch' with Floppy while Biplob and Avantika dipped their toes in the stream.

After a couple of hours, Biplob yawned "Lets head back, if we leave now we can meet farmer Balram for lunch."

They quickly packed everything. Addy refilled their water bottles from the stream, as Avantika stuffed their haversacks with the sandwich wrappers, ensuring that no litter was left back. The meadow looked exactly as it was when they first got there!

As they passed Jaggu's garden, they found him standing crestfallen, clutching a spray – can, his moustache drooping.

"Is everything alright?" asked Biplob, concerned.

"You've cursed my garden!" wailed Jaggu, "After you left, strange insects have attacked my plants. Even the strongest pesticide has no effect on them."

"How rude!" said Avantika, "We've come to help and you're blaming us instead!" Biplob muttered, "Hmmm. Very interesting."

Jaggu complained indignantly, "Interesting?! How insensitive!"

"You dare call Biplob insensitive!" exclaimed Addy as Floppy let out small growls.

"Relax everyone," said Biplob, "What's interesting is this is an attack of Tomato Hornworms".

"Rubbish!" said Farmer Jaggu, "They've not only attacked the tomatoes but even the brinjals and potatoes."

"Tomato Hornworms destroy tomato, potato and brinjal plants!" explained Biplob, "And though that pesticide won't work, there's a perfectly natural solution for this problem!"

Biplob quickly reeled off instructions, “Addy, fill the spray – can with detergent and water. Avantika, fetch some pepper.”

Jaggu looked on bewildered as they quickly followed Biplob’s instructions. “Now spray the detergent solution all over the plants Addy,” continued Biplob.

“What about me?” asked Avantika. “Sprinkle pepper on the plants that Addy has already sprayed,” replied Biplob.

Floppy followed, wagging his tail like he was supervising them!

“We’ll soon rid you of this hornworm problem Farmer Jaggu,” explained Biplob, “The detergent solution makes the tomato hornworms fall off and pepper ensures they don’t return!”

Once they were done, the garden was littered with fallen tomato hornworms!

Farmer Jaggu sheepishly thanked them for their help, “My garden is always open for you Biplob.” Soon, they were on their way home.

"You helped him even though he blamed you for the hornworm attack Biplob?" wondered Addy.

"An eye for an eye will make the world blind!" explained Biplob, "If I'm nasty to him too, this vicious cycle will continue forever. It is better to help each other. After all, if his garden is healthy, that's good for him and for all of us!" as they reached home for a well – earned lunch!

About the Author

Abhishek Talwar (AIEMA), a certified environmentalist, has the gift of narrating difficult concepts with simplicity and fun. This ease of narrative, combined with the values of love for the environment, loyalty and friendship that shine through each story make these books truly entertaining and enriching for children.

About the Illustrator

Sonal Goyal completed her masters in fine arts from College of Art, Delhi. Having been creative head at a leading publishing house, she is now an independent artist. Her love for drawing and books has led her to creating cute and lovable illustrations that spread smiles.

BIPLOB WORLD

Published by Ritika Talwar

ISBN 978-81-947094-7-3
Typeset in Sabon LT Std Roman

www.biplobworld.com

Dedicated to my loving wife, Ritika, for always believing. And to my curious children, for inspiring these tales.

BIPLOB THE BUMBLEBEE
Book Series

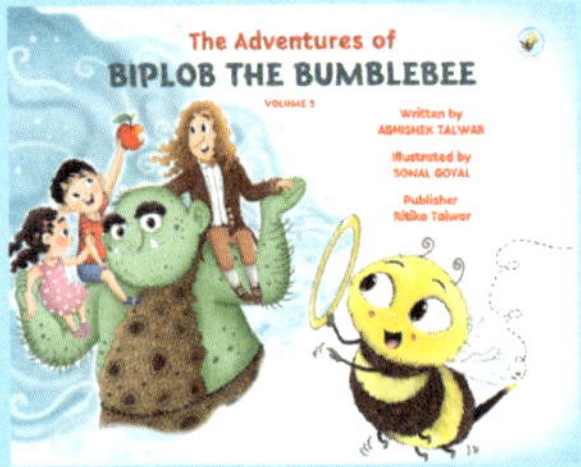

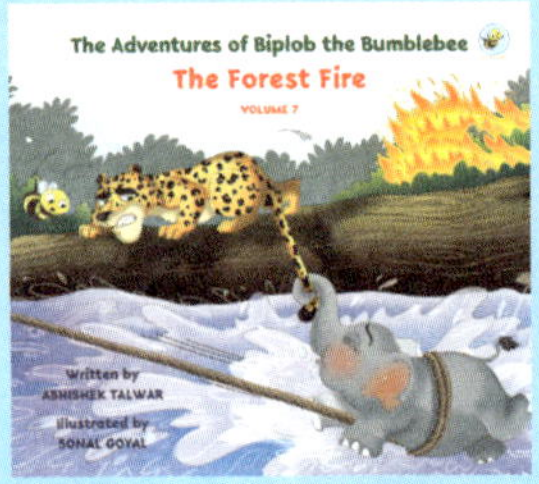

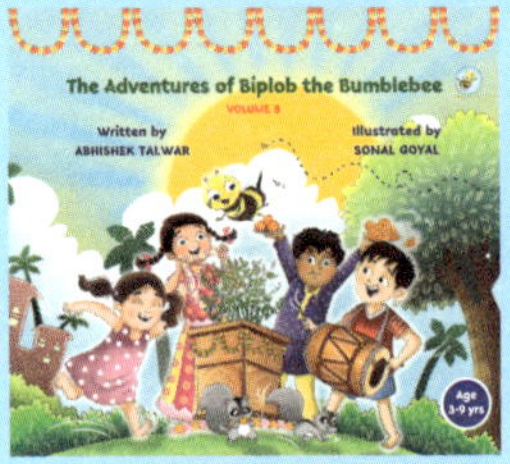

Scan to Order Now